Sad, Black, and Fat:

Musings From The Intersection

By Tangela Williams-Spann

fruitful.poetic.light
Published Co.

To contact the author:
Tangela Williams-Spann
6800 Clarita St.
East St. Louis, IL 62207
tspannwrites@gmail.com
Instagram: @twillspann
Twitter: @twillspann
Website: http://twillspannwrites.com

Published by fruitful.poetic.light, LLC
fruitful.poetic.light@gmail.com
www.fruitfulpoeticlight.com
Instagram: @fruitful.poetic.light
Facebook: https://www.facebook.com/fruitful.poetic.light

ISBN-13: 9780578901183 (pb)

Cover design by: Kerry Watson, fiverr.com
Printed in the United States of America

Sad, Black, and Fat

CONTENTS

Mental Break

Part 3: FAT

Introduction

Blank Spaces

I've wanted to be a writer my whole life.

Sure, I've had other career plans: cowboy, pharmacist, archer, etc.; but, I've wanted to write consistently the entire time. I even wanted to major in journalism when I started college. Feels forever ago now.

This online thing is nice, but nothing beats pen and paper in my book. Pretty pens and nice stationery get me all excited. I guess the words have more meaning if I write them down. A kind of old magic, I think. Saying things aloud gives words power, but writing them down gives them more strength.

I have had lots of journals over the years. Hardcover; softcover; hell, even loose-leaf. My early writing consisted mostly of random daily thoughts and some poems. In middle school, I entered one of them in a contest and won second place or at least that's how I remember it.

I've tried to keep up with all of my writing over the years, but life has the ability to get in the way from time to time. For example, in high school, there was a blue binder I used to have that was full of my writing. Inside, there was also a draft of a play I was working on. Now that I think about it, my idea would have worked better as a novel. I had several notebooks full of doodles and drabbles that never grew bigger than a few sentences. I tended to get a few pages into a new notebook and promptly lose it. I was a scatterbrain back in the day. I left a lot of my stuff at my mother's place when I moved out at 23. That house was consumed by fire in 2009. Things I believed that I could always come back to were lost forever. It was a difficult thing to accept, but such is life.

Time passed and I kept writing. Fanfiction was a way I could work on my craft and get out some of my fangirl feelings. I wrote stories about the X-Men and Bleach for years. I even wrote a few erotic stories (Those feelings needed to get out too, you know). They're still available online if you ever want to read them, but I don't think I'll go back and finish. My heart just isn't in it anymore. Marvel is trash and Bleach is finished, the show's over.

I have a habit of collecting journals. Pretty ones, those that are eye catching. I'm always hard-pressed to not purchase one when I see it. I have lots of them just sitting on shelves in my space. Totally empty. Untouched since I bought them. It bothers me from time to time. I used to have so many stories to tell; so many words that I needed to get out before they escaped me permanently. Now, I'm lucky if I manage to get a hundred words put together every day. Being surrounded by all these empty pages is kind of like being reminded of my shortcomings. I bought these things with ideas in mind for them; ideas that have faded into the ether of my memories. I have mental illness to thank for that, but I've been using that as an excuse for too long.

My goal for myself is to stop being passive with my writing; to stop being lazy and letting my ideas fade away. It doesn't matter anymore about how poorly organized they are or how depressing they might be. It doesn't even matter if they never form into a real story. I have to keep flexing my creative muscle or it will die. It's come close a few times already. Losing my ability to use words is something I couldn't live with.

One of my goals for this book is to help. Some of this book will be a little hard to take. This journey has not been all sunshine and roses, but it is honest.

I know mental health is taboo in the Black community. People aren't willing to have the discussions about how we all struggle. It gets waved away with declarations of "That's for white folks" or "That's just the devil talking." My personal favorite is, "You better depress your ass in there and get that laundry done," or some other similar threats.

I'm hoping that my honesty helps to normalize talking about mental health with Black folks. If people can see my vulnerability, they will realize that speaking about their troubles and perhaps even seeking professional help is the healthy and correct action to take in their lives.

I'm putting all this into the universe. Stepping out on Faith, as the church ladies say. Writing it down and giving the words the power again. I'm finally ready to do the work. I'm ready to watch doors open in front of me. I'm ready to move forward.

Part 1

SAD

Get it out

I write because I need to.
I don't mean that metaphorically.
I literally need to.
My emotional stability depends on it.
I get sad when I can't get my thoughts out. My own self-talk poisons me into a horrible depressive state that nothing but time can alleviate.
Time and words.
I have words.
I always have.
I was gifted with my ability to use them.
So many beautiful, elaborate, dreamy words.
Sometimes, they're healthy.
Other times, not so much.
They beg for escape.
Pounding on the walls of my mind until I set them free or choke them back.
I've lost track of so many lovely words, simply because I refused to give them free reign.
Story ideas, feelings I needed to express.
All gone back into the recesses of my imagination.
Sometimes they come back in snippets, but never as fully formed as the original emergence.
I've decided to stop letting them escape.
I'm writing everything down now.
Keeping my words restrained isn't healthy.
I've taken years to come to terms with this. I've wasted a lot of time keeping my words cooped up like so many chickens.
But I'm done with that now.
There are things I want to say.
Things I may or may not be able to say aloud.

Messages that I need to get across.
They may not matter to anyone else, but they are important to me.
Everyone has an opinion on everything.
Myself included.
I used to keep that opinion to myself for various reasons.
Fear. Insecurity.
Not wanting to make waves.
Those days are behind me.
My personal philosophy is to be like water.
Water is deep.
Water is calming.
Water is flexible.
If I'm being like water…
Swift. Resilient. Powerful.
I have to embrace all of its forms. The flowing river and the raging torrent.
I've been calm for long enough.
It's tsunami time.
I'm ready to start making waves again.

Honesty Hour

Gonna be honest.
I don't have anything left in the tank.
I'm drained.
I'm tired.
I'm beyond done.
If I could just leave, that would be wonderful.
I would start walking and never look back. I could drop everything right now.
I feel as if my world likes to shift its axis every so often.
Just when I think, for half a moment, that everything is okay or things will be fine.
BLOOP!
Next thing I know, I'm scrambling for answers again.
That's what my optimism has gotten me.
This is where I am. This is where I have been for some time.
For the record.
In case anyone was wondering.

Doing the Most

I have been thinking about my productivity quite a bit. I feel like I should be doing more.
My students should be learning more.
I should be working harder in school.
My house should be cleaner.
My family could be happier.
At the same time, I know I'm doing all I can right now.
I feel like I have two jobs on permanent rotation.
One I get paid for
And one I don't.
Working in special education drains you in a way that I believe no one could prepare you for.
Although, when I need a break from my work kids, I can take it if I really need to.
Once I clock out in the afternoon, I have to get my mind ready for my second shift.
My family needs me to have my senses about me.
I can't get a sick day from them.
I can't claim that I need a mental health day.
Even though I so desperately need it at times.
Being in college is still a trip.
Deadlines are deadlines and things need to get done.
I can't half-ass anything either.
You will get called out on it. It can be overwhelming, even if you don't have other obligations to deal with.
It never feels like enough. I run myself ragged and it isn't enough.
No wonder people flip out and go on shooting sprees.
People are tired,
weary in spirit,
and have no real outlet.

4

Myself included.

Am I going to flip out and have a serious episode? Probably not. I have a son to get through college.

Sometimes, though.

Just sometimes...

It can be fun to think about.

Late-Nighter

I need to write more.

I've read about other writers that have set writing times each day. A specific amount of time set aside each day to put words on the page. I feel like this would work well for me.

The only issue is finding the time. I already get up pretty early for work. Then, I'm off educating young minds for a good portion of the day. After that, I have to figure out food for the family and do some studying. If I manage to stay awake for that, I could get some writing done, but it's hard to be inspired when you can barely function.

I used to get a lot of creative writing done late at night. I would stay up and hammer out all kinds of stories. A lot of it was fanfiction, but I was still writing. Almost all of my multi-chapter stories were written, edited, or published after midnight. My ideas tend to flow better around 2 a.m.

This was back before I had to be coherent before 6 a.m. every day. When staying awake didn't have any repercussions. Things are much different now.

I think my brain is slowly making adjustments. Finding space in between the fissures and cracks of time where I am able to actually formulate a concept from the imaginary. I've been taken away by several little ideas during my work hours. My fairy tale story is piecing itself together slowly. This tale will either include a princess or several elemental creatures. They won't leave me alone. I don't always have the time to stop what I'm doing and write down my thoughts and when I lose an idea it is often hard to recall later and that's the real tragedy here.

When I'm too sad to think, writing is out of the question. I can barely stop hating myself to carry out life's basic functions. So, you can forget anything creative. What a waste of time. Also, winter and the holiday season are usually the hardest for me. I get stuck in some real, unpleasant feelings. As a result, I can't write and I feel bad about not writing which makes me not write more and that makes me feel worse.

And so on and so on and so on…

The Floor Isn't Lava

As I lay on the floor crying my only thought was; "What the hell are you doing?"

I probably shouldn't have been on the floor. It's hard and it makes your ribs hurt if you lay there too long. No one should spend any serious time on the floor without sex or yoga or both involved. Regardless, that was where I found myself. My mind managed to convince me that not only did I deserve to be on the floor, I should stay there for half an hour.

My son found me first. He sat down next to me and asked if I was okay. I told him I wasn't and he rubbed my back for a while. When he was bored, he turned on the Xbox and started playing Sonic Generations. One of the better Sonic Games, if I do say so myself. Considering he's autistic and empathy isn't his strong suit, I'm glad he managed to care about my pain for that long. I probably scared him.

Eventually, my son went and told my husband I was laying on the floor. He came in and talked me into laying on our bed. It's much more comfortable than the floor. I cried and apologized until I fell asleep. He listened and assured me that I had nothing to be sorry about.

This is the part where I'm supposed to talk about overcoming my mental illness. I'm supposed to say that days like this are few and far between and that I'm getting better every day.

Surprise! This isn't the case.

Depression and I have been very close buds since around 13. My days are always dampened by my personal raincloud that follows me. Some days I can force it into submission. There are days when I can laugh and joke with the best of them and nobody would even suspect that I was perpetually miserable. Other days, I am much less pleasant to be around.

8

Black people, Black women in particular, aren't allowed to show any kind of weakness. You are leaving yourself open to attack if you do. My family members were not good examples of how to mentally take care of myself. The only emotions that my mother ever displayed publicly were either anger or indifference. My father was an expert at muted silence that erupted into loud raging. My mother's two sisters were each stunning examples of how to not address bipolar disorder and schizophrenia respectively. I didn't want to be lumped into the raging bitch category either, so I shoved my feelings down and tried not to feel anything. It helped along the way towards my goal of not wanting to be any trouble if nobody realized I was there.

Spoiler! That shit is hella harmful.

Not allowing your feelings the space to exist is a form of self-harm in my mind. You are human and your emotions are part of you. They are there for a reason and they are valid. You cannot escape them. If you keep stuffing them down, they will manifest in another way. Strokes, heart attacks and other illnesses related to stress spring to mind.

Like Solange said, "You gotta let it go."

I like to vent online but you have to be careful with that as well. I spend hours online with all manner of triggering stories presented to me in the media. Anytime a black person is killed by the police, I have to take a little internet break. No social media and no news. I would lose myself in grief otherwise. I consider myself an empath and I've become very good at absorbing emotions that aren't really mine. The week featuring the Alton Sterling and Philando Castile killings was particularly hellish for me.

It's not as if I haven't tried to get help. I've been in therapy and on various meds on and off for about fifteen years. I would feel like I could manage on my own and stop taking the medication when I was younger. I wouldn't always go to my therapy appointments. Sometimes, I felt like I didn't need to. Other times, my paranoia kept me from wanting to talk to my therapist. Eventually, I would end up in "Relapse City" and I would feel worse than before.

I don't have great coping skills and I used to take a lot of mental health days off from work. I never lost a job because of it but my work performance was terrible. On the days I would show up, people could tell that I was going through the motions. I've gotten better at faking "okayness" over the years. I force myself out of bed and down the highway to work nearly every day. I wear my mask and make nice with my coworkers. I bet only one or two could ever guess I was depressed. They were probably doing the same thing I was, just getting by.

I'm back on the wagon for the time being. I'm taking my medicine daily and have started talking to a therapist online. It's not the same format that I'm used to, but I like the informal framework. I can take my time with responding without being judged and it's cheaper than going to sit in a clinician's office once a week. If you are having problems with finding someone to talk to locally, there are several online options to choose from.

Every day is a struggle and I've accepted that. I can't promise that I won't end up on the floor again because Summer is coming and the floor is much cooler. As long as I manage to pick myself up again, I'll be fine.

One day at a time.

Wedding Day Blues

The days leading up to my wedding day were the most stressful I have experienced in my entire adult life. I know the same rings true for many people, but this is how it went:

About 48 hours before the ceremony, there was a huge storm. There had been a tornado warning in effect but nothing officially touched down in our area. There were terrifying wind gusts, a significant amount of hail, and lots of flash flooding. The storm hit just before dusk and we couldn't fully see the all of the damage until the next day, However, a fallen tree knocked a telephone pole onto our house. Power lines were down and we couldn't get inside our home for the night. Power was out all over town. It was scary and frustrating. We spent the night on my aunt's couch and didn't sleep a wink.

The following day, power had not been restored and we had to rescue all the food for the wedding from the powerless church. We had been planning on getting things ready in the church's kitchen so we would have less work in transporting food and wedding supplies. Sadly, the power outage changed the situation. Everything had to be prepared at my mother's house, which was nowhere near as accommodating as a commercial kitchen.

My husband-to-be spent most of the day making sure our house wasn't too heavily damaged. The fallen tree had to be removed before the power company would repair the lines. My father and a couple of the other men in the neighborhood spent the morning cutting up logs and clearing debris from around the block. Thankfully, though a little banged up, there wasn't any significant damage to our home.

Later that evening, the power came back and my family and I rushed to get the decorating finished for the wedding the next day. I couldn't see how everything was going to get finished on time and I cried most of the night.

At some point during our mad decorating frenzy, my fiancé was kidnapped by his groomsmen for a surprise bachelor party and I didn't see him again until the next morning. There was still a lot to be done and they just took off. I was furious beyond words and practically hysterical. I hadn't been that angry with him before or since and I remember being dangerously close to calling the whole thing off. I realized later that it wasn't really his fault, but it still stung at the time. I never got to have a bachelorette party. I had planning, work, and stress. The unfairness of it all wasn't helping my anxiety.

The next day, my husband and I bought a small tree to be planted during the ceremony. We spent most of the morning at a local nursery searching for something we could later plant in our yard. I never found something that really spoke to me, but we settled on a crepe myrtle at the last second and rushed to the church for the ceremony.

We got to the church just in time for the photographer to call and say that he was lost. He was driving in from an hour away and had gotten turned around on the interstate. I was livid. How could someone get lost on their way to their job? In this age of smartphones and GPS, there was no excuse. He was almost too late for the wedding and he got there about 30 minutes before showtime. There was a mad rush to get pregame photos and I still felt like nothing good would come from any of this.

I was concerned about our ceremony taking place outside. We had planned to use the back field of the church because the view from the top of the hill was gorgeous. I was worried about the ground being too soft after a storm from two nights before. The bridesmaids and myself were going to be barefoot and nobody wanted muddy toes. Fortunately, things had dried up beautifully and we could proceed as planned.

The ceremony started and after walking down the aisle, I notice that our tree wasn't where it should be. It was easy to notice that an extra tree was missing from our little setup in the backyard of the church. After some harsh whispering while the preacher was talking, my cousin comes running around the building with the tree. It must have been at least thirty pounds of plant and soil he was carrying. He was hauling that stuff like a linebacker headed for the end zone. Funny now, but it wasn't amusing at the time.

Later, the photographer wanted to take pictures of my husband and I. We were delayed in coming to the reception and people got antsy. My mother decided to feed them early and lots of them ate and ran. By the time my husband and I got back, about two-thirds of our guests were gone. People were starting to clean up the reception hall and we barely had any food left for us. I was a wreck.

I know everyone has a wedding day story, but I think mine is a doozy. This is an abbreviated version because of time and memory and it still makes me anxious to think about it.

Also, if you are planning a wedding, don't. Do yourself a favor and hire someone to handle things for you. Your experience will be much more pleasant that way.

I'm Not Interested In Your Baby, Lady

This is another essay about my hang-ups. Particularly, my hang-up with having babies.

Don't get me wrong, I like the idea of babies. Most babies are cute and give people hope for the future. Being around newborns makes a lot of women get the *I want one* urge; myself included. I squashed that nonsense with a quickness. I don't hate babies; I just don't want another one. I have my reasons. These reasons stem from a previous relationship with the Ex. I won't use his name; he doesn't deserve it.

The whole story is kind of long and involved, but here's the highly abridged version. We were together for around two years. He started truck driving and a lot of that time he was away. My family hated him so to avoid conflict, I kept our relationship a secret. This often involved sneaking around like a covert operative to maintain the strained connection that we had.

Bottom line is, I got pregnant. For some odd reason, he didn't believe that I was pregnant. He flat out refused to acknowledge it. I charge this disbelief to the bad messaging he was receiving from his friends. They never had any love for me and were high key racist. I'm sure they convinced him that I was trying to scam him in some way. He broke up with me a few weeks after I told him about the baby.

This hurt. This betrayal. The person I was sure I would spend the rest of my days with no longer cared about me. Not only that, the revelation that he was perfectly fine with abandoning the new life we had inadvertently created together stung. I wasn't sure how to cope.

Part of this story is that I'd never wanted kids. Not even when I was little. Then, all of a sudden, I'm left pregnant and alone. It was extremely traumatic for me. I made some dangerous and questionable decisions out of grief and heartbrokenness. I spent Super Bowl week of 2004 in a psych ward on suicide watch and I only remember feeling angry, frustrated, and terrified the entire time I was pregnant.

I didn't see or hear from him again until my son was two months old. I ran into him at a gas station. We briefly exchanged pleasantries while pumping gas. I asked how things were going and He shrugged non-committedly. He asked how I'd been and I responded in kind. My little one was sleeping in the car seat. I don't think he ever saw the baby. He didn't ask and I didn't show.

The pregnancy was normal and my son was a healthy newborn, but I can never let myself go through having another child. I know the situation would be different and I wouldn't have to go through it alone, but I can't make it okay in my mind. It's an ugly spot in my marriage. There was a point when we couldn't even talk about having more children without me crying. I have gotten better over time. I can talk about it now, but it's still uncomfortable. I even have a hard time when other people tell me about their pregnancies. It's extremely irritating.

I hate it when people give me a hard time about having another kid. Just because I'm married, that isn't reason enough for me to start breeding as soon as possible. There are enough little ones in the world without people to love on them. My situation would be different, certainly, but I don't need to add another hungry belly to my household.

My husband is amazing about the whole thing and I feel really guilty. He doesn't have any kids of his own and would be more than happy to have a baby. I just can't do it. He doesn't like how hurt I am over the whole situation and I know he's frustrated too. We don't bring it up very often, but it always feels like a dark cloud over our whole relationship.

Anyway.

If you are one of those ladies that enjoys being pregnant, I tip my hat to you. It's not for me. I can't promise that I won't side-eye you whenever you start talking about how fulfilled and beautiful you feel. I did it once; I know the game.

Also, don't get offended if I stay fifteen feet away from your glorious, shiny newborns. I swear it's not them, it's me.

Daydreams

Depression sucks.

It has this thing it likes to do, normally when I mentally have my guard down for a bit, it imagines worst-case scenarios for my family and I. I could be driving along and suddenly...

What if your husband gets hurt in a car wreck? What if he doesn't come home?

or

What if you get sick? Cancer runs in the family. What will become of you?

And for unknown reasons, my imagination allows this to play out in my head. Over and over again until I'm miserable. I can fight it off some days, but not all of them.

It's scary that my brain can manage that kind of sadism. Self-inflicted sadism at that.

I'm sick.

Ebb

Depression is a weird thing. It manifests in so many ways. There are the common symptoms: Lack of energy; lack of interest; lethargy; lack of focus. Some folks throw themselves into something in an attempt to avoid their feelings.

"I don't have time to stay in bed, I have a deadline."

"I can't eat. I have more important things to do."

"I forgot to do something important. I have to push myself harder next time."

These folks don't seem outwardly depressed. In fact, they seem like very productive and together people. If you look closely, these same folks are trying to bury something that could ultimately kill them. They tend to burn out fast and their crash is worse because of the overwork.

Just because people seem on top of things on the outside, doesn't mean that inwardly they're not falling apart.

Dream Babies

I had a long, unsettling dream this morning.

In the first part, I was pregnant. My mother and some of my work friends were planning a baby shower. They were telling my husband that he couldn't come. To his credit, my love was having none of it. He was full-on arguing with the ladies about his right to be there. It was sweet.

Later, my husband and I were getting an ultrasound. The tech was moving the sensor around on my belly and I swear I could feel it. Cold gel and everything. Eventually, the tech pointed to a screen and showed us not one, but two babies. As he offered us congratulations, I felt a panic attack beginning to build up in my chest. I was unprepared for two babies.

I dream about babies a lot. The old ladies say that dreaming about babies means that one is on the way and I've always rebuked that narrative. At the same time, I am visited by a number of little souls, clamoring for me to be their mamma.

One dream featured a chubby-cheeked little darling that was a snuggler. A beautiful, dark-skinned child with lots of hair. I couldn't put him down without him issuing a whimper that would melt the ice around anyone's heart. I carried him around for the entire dream and he nuzzled into my neck. His name was Isaac Isaiah.

Another dream featured an older girl. She had a brighter complexion and hazel eyes. I can't remember exactly what she said her name was, but I remember it was different. Marigold, I believe. I called her Maggie for short.

Maggie and I were walking somewhere. I think I was walking her to school. She held my hand and talked about everything and nothing. She smiled a lot and so did I. I did my best to answer all her questions, but I can't remember what they were anymore.

The twins visit me too. Always a boy and a girl. They are usually infants when I find them. I haven't had a dream that featured them specifically apart from the pregnancy one. They linger around the fringes of my consciousness at times. I'm aware that they are there, but they never present themselves totally. They tease me, the scamps.

I've talked about my reluctance to get pregnant again before. There's a lot of unresolved feelings associated with pregnancy and it isn't something I really want. However, my husband doesn't have any children and I feel a little guilty about being so unwilling.

There was a long period that we couldn't even discuss it. My first pregnancy was emotionally traumatic and I'm still trying to heal from it. I've made large strides but I'm still too afraid to let it happen again. I keep telling myself that it would be okay one day, but I'm not getting any younger. My window is slowly closing.

He would be an amazing baby daddy. I know he's a great parent to the son we have now. However, having a newborn is a different challenge. He would have to learn how to nurture a brand-new person. Teaching him about the "breast is best" debate would be amusing. Diaper changing too. I don't think he's ever had to change a poopy pamper in his life. My love has never had to wash vomit off a toddler while assuring them that things were okay. I think the experience would change his thoughts about parenthood entirely.

That isn't to say it won't ever happen. The Lord moves in mysterious ways. I, however, know that I am doing what I can to prevent it from happening.

Newborns, in this economy? Are you crazy?

Dear Tangie,

Hey, Sis.
It's me. Us, rather.

I know it's been hard. Life just keeps throwing haymakers.
And we are no boxer, We'll take the knockdown. Life is hard,
I get it.
Take your time to feel your feelings. I'm not saying to never
get down. But we need to stand up again now. Things are
gonna be okay.
There are a lot of things swirling inside your head. This
anxiety is a trip. However, you are strong enough to handle
it. You are equipped with everything you need; just step into
your God given power.
If it is meant for you, then it's already yours. Get up and take
it.
Relax. Stop stressing about things out of your hands. We are
going to be fine. Your physical health is starting to wear down
from stress. Stop worrying about it and take care of it. You're
better than this. You have people than need you. Don't waste
away in your own personal dungeons.
Please. For us?
For me?

Love,
Tangie

Be Present

It's Back to School Eve for me again! It's just as anxiety-inducing for teachers as it is for the kids. This time last year, I spent the day coloring with my son and relaxing. Today, I've got some appointments to keep. Booked and busy, as they say.

People are going to ask how my summer went. I always have issues with coming up with an answer. I spent most of my summer on the couch, watching *The Office* and YouTube. Didn't really travel. Nothing very exciting. It was fine, but not much to talk about. I'm not sure what type of stories people are expecting, but I don't have them.

I could talk about how I've been struggling, physically and mentally. I could let people know how many times I've cried to my therapist. I could let people know how cranky I've been with my husband. I could tell people how guilty I feel for taking my hard-earned two months of couch time because I'm not getting paid. I could let people know how close to being on the street two months without a paycheck left me. I doubt people would be into that. So, instead, I'll play nice. I'll be pleasant and make small talk. I'd rather not, but that's what people do.

Today, I'm going to remember my peace. I need to remember that work is going to be fine. Business as usual. Nothing to be nervous or irritated about. Nothing to lose any more sleep worrying about.

Today's mantra: "I'm going to be present for today's things today and worry about tomorrow's things tomorrow."

Scrooge

Today, I got cornered by a woman who was way into Christmas. We were waiting to check out at Walmart. She had a cart full of decorations and made sure to tell me how excited she was about the holidays and how her husband already had the lights up and how she did the tree Thanksgiving night. She obviously couldn't tell how uncomfortable I was even though I kept dropping my bags of Reese's Pieces.

At some point, she managed to ask if I had my tree up already and I politely explained that I don't really care for Christmas. The poor thing looked appalled and asked if I was "one of those Jewish types" and said that "the other thing they do with the candles looks fun."

I was past politeness at this point. I told her that I'm not Jewish, although Hanukkah does seem lovely and that my crippling depression makes most days, including holidays, suck balls. It was kinda funny how flustered she got. I switched lines and paid for my candy in peace.

The nerve of some people.

Lay down your burdens

I'll be the first to admit, I have trouble with Christianity. There are a lot of so-called Christians that have turned me off towards organized religion.

"You need to go to church."

"You need to pay your tithes."

"You can't dress like that here."

"You can't bring that heathen in here with you."

Their nasty behavior and judgmental attitudes are disgusting and I don't have the energy for such treatment.

Despite being raised in the Baptist church, I don't identify with any religion. I've gotten the most out of Buddhist teachings in my adult life, but I'm not strictly aligned with them either. I believe that life is full of suffering and that people can't escape it. A mindset change is a way to get through your life.

I don't think the Divine needs all the pomp and circumstance. It's there. I know it is. It knows I'm here. I respect it. We have an understanding. It doesn't take any grand ceremony to marvel at the Universe's handiwork. From microcosms to galaxies, it's there if you care to look and be amazed.

But I digress...

Over the past several days, things have been less than great for me. I've been down and extra stressed. I know finals week had a lot to do with it, but still. My prayer has been for the strength to get through the end of the year with a peaceful mind.

Heaven knows, it has been less than calm lately.

I'm not typically a praying person, but I talked to the Universe for a bit last night. I cried and vented and asked for grace. It felt good to let go of some of the feelings I was keeping bottled up. Honestly, I felt a little lighter when I finished.

Today, I had a pretty good day of work. Things didn't feel as rushed or as hectic as they had been. I can't say I'm not grateful. Small victories are still victories.

Relapse

This time last year, I was happy and in love. I wrote a sappy post for the man I loved and was glad to share it with the world. Yesterday, I felt amazing; I was all set to put another sappy post into the universe. For the first time in ages, I felt as if I was doing something good for my life. It seemed like things were going to be okay and I was moving in the right direction.

Today is a different story...

Maybe it's because I had a weird dream about my dead grandfather.

Maybe it was because I didn't get my extra walk in today.

Maybe it was because my stress level peaked again this afternoon.

Maybe because today is my anniversary and my personal life is lowkey in shambles.

Maybe because I blew my calorie budget in an attempt to make myself feel better and the food was mediocre at best.

Maybe it was because I'm not allowed to be in a decent mood for any significant amount of time.

Either way, right now I'm feeling terrible about myself. About my life. About my future. My depression has returned with a vengeance. I hate when this happens. It's as if I dared to imagine my life without this heaviness on my heart. It's like I offended my illness and it's angry. It is being needlessly relentless today.

No, depression. I didn't forget about you. I would love to, but I can't. You don't give me a chance to. You don't leave me alone for long enough for me to escape you long term. You know that, don't you?

Don't You?

Voyage

adrift.

floating along silently.

moving only as the waves decide

voices call from the shore

turn your head

fill your ears with liquid

the water is cold

but also calming

no need to fear

the sun is bright

blinding. burning.

eyes close to avoid the glare

skin still burns

still hurts

drifting further

       further

SAD, BLACK, AND FAT

further

               away from the shore

Toss-Up

Recently, I've spent far too much time watching the sunrise. I don't have an issue with this most of the time. Sunlight helps me fight depression. At the same time, anxious sleepless nights have become my new normal. I'm always awake when daybreak happens and I don't want to disturb anyone's rest, so I lie in bed and watch the light break across the windows.

Mornings can be very nice. Running through your morning routine every day can help a person feel focused and on track. Sadly, I'm not one of those people.

When I have to get up early for work or some other engagement, there are days when I'm too full of anxiety about the upcoming day to rest properly. I'm upset when the alarm goes off. I drag myself to get ready and make my son do the same. We have to be out the door at a certain time, you know.

It's easy to set yourself on autopilot when you have other things to think about. Your daily schedule can be an excellent distraction from whatever emotional nonsense the brain might be preparing to unleash. The days when I don't have the distraction are more interesting to me.

My brain hasn't settled on a course yet, so my feelings can fluctuate between ready to go and ready to stay in bed. I might have a really good day or a terrible one. It could honestly go either way. I can feel both in turn, fighting for control. Telling myself that I'm going to be okay only works occasionally. To be honest, I don't feel as if it's my decision. I could be determined to feel one thing and end up in a totally different emotional place. It just depends. The process can be alarmingly exhausting.

Does any of this sound familiar? Do other people's depression and anxiety have a battle with them every day? I'm sure I'm not alone in this. Is it any wonder why people seem so frustrated and stressed first thing in the morning? Dealing with yourself can be a daunting daily event. Couple that with the normal stress of living in our society and the dangerous setup for burnout and emotional collapse is set into motion. Is it any wonder why there have been so many attacks at schools and workplaces in America? People are stretched thin.

I don't have an overarching solution. It's difficult for me to find answers for myself sometimes. The difference between myself and others is that I'm slowly trying to break the cycle. Many people just keep pushing until something gives. Usually meaning that their physical health or personal relationships suffer as a result. I've done that too many times in the past and it is no way to live.

Lately, I've been trying to pay attention to myself and when I can tell that I'm approaching a breaking point, I want to find a good way to slow down. It's difficult but possible. I'm not always successful, but I'm still learning.

We all are...

Don't Stop here/Now what?

Depression is tiring.

One wouldn't think that with the general impression of a depressed person being someone who lays around all the time, not doing anything. The fight is internal, hence the "invisible illness" designation.

For example, I don't want to leave the house most of the time. Going out of my room can be a struggle. There are days that I'll just stay on or near my bed. Taking care of myself is a monumental task that is just too much for me to handle. I won't eat, won't drink; just existing and thinking.

That's what other people see, but in my head, there's a battle going on. I have to convince myself that staying alive is a good idea. I have to convince myself that I deserve happiness and that things are going to be fine. I have to remember that I'm important to others and that I am loved. All the while, my brain is assuring me that I am unworthy; that I'm wretched and incapable of functioning like a normal person. Many days, my brain wins and I'm stuck in the endless sadness cycle.

The same battle is always going on, even on days when I seem okay. The days when I can smile and laugh at my family's silly jokes. Days where I can go to work without a problem. Days when I seem like an amazing person to be around. My brain is still telling me that I suck and am a waste of space and stardust. I can fight it off, but it's difficult.

Medication helps. It gets me out the door many days. Once I'm out, however, I'm on my own. I have to manage my mood to be a functional member of society. I can have several good days in a row, but the shadow of a down spell is always looming. At any moment, the pendulum could swing and I'll be a sad sack again.

I can feel when it happens. Stopping it is impossible and it feels awful.

Being back on a daytime schedule has only reminded me that I have to stay strong. Some people depend on me to be a force for good in their lives. They need to know that things are going to be okay, one way or another.

So, I wake up every day and keep fighting. Not for my sake, but for theirs. I'm lucky enough to have that in my life.

It's my reason to keep going.

I'm right up against graduation now. About a month and a half away. Three more classes to finish in that time. I'm shopping around for decent online graduate programs.

I should be congratulating myself. I put in a lot of hard work and long hours to get where I am, and I should be proud.

To a degree, I am. I never thought I would get here. I would just be enrolled in undergrad indefinitely. It's taken this long. Why wouldn't it always be there?

Somehow, I've put together enough hours for someone to decide that I need to get out of there. One hundred and seventy-seven credit hours amassed since 2001 to be precise.

I've wasted a lot of time on failure. Thinking about it. Obsessing over it. Feeling like I wasn't good enough for success. It created a bunch of false starts and premature stops. I failed some classes and bounced around schools. When I went back full time in 2011, I decided that I wasn't dropping the ball anymore. I wouldn't stop working until I had a bachelor's degree of some kind in my possession. I didn't care what kind or who it came from. I just needed it to be finished.

Fast forward to now. I'm really on the edge of achieving a major life goal. At a time when I should be elated and proud, I'm facing another big unknown.

Now what?

That's the question that plagues so many of us. You've pushed so long and so hard for something and the Fates decided to be kind and bless you. Now what?

What will you do with your energy now? What about all that resolve? What will you devote yourself to?

I've found myself at a crossroads and I'm feeling lost. I honestly have no idea of what to do with myself now.

I've asked for advice. People tell me to pursue something I love. They ask where I see myself in five or ten years. It's hard because I never allow myself to dream. I don't let myself look forward to very much. I can't handle disappointment very well. Basically, I'd given up on wanting more for myself. That's part of why I am so unprepared for the future. I never really faced it. I've been so focused on getting through every single day that I couldn't even imagine what could be.

In five years, I'll be forty years old. In the land that people call middle-aged. My son will be done with high school and I'll have an empty nest. That's when people are supposed to start enjoying life, right? After their kids are grown.

I could have a master's degree in something by then. That sounds cool.

I could find a career I could throw myself into. Try to make a difference in the world.

I could say to hell with this, buy an RV, and drive around North America.

All very realistic options.

In the meantime, I'm trying to let myself be hopeful about my life. About where I've been and where I'm going. I've begun to stick my head out from under my cloud to see what I've been missing all these years. I must trust that I'm making the right decisions and that I've learned from my bad ones. I'm looking ahead for the first time in years, just to find a gaping void. A void full of potential options and outcomes stands before me and it's terrifying.

Now what, indeed?

Part 2

BLACK

Make a Change

Words, my friends, have power.

The things that people say and even implied messages have such a huge effect on us. It's a miracle that we can process anything with all the language that we are receiving daily. This includes: advertising, media, and so on. I don't know how many times the media has shown me that people that look like me aren't valuable and important. Enough to internalize some things, I can tell you that.

It happens to all of us. We can use the most terrible things to validate our own destructive feelings. Snide comments at work. Ugly tirades in articles. Less than positive visuals. It all goes back to the messages we chose to let in and those we do not.

I wonder why so many people are thoughtless with their words and actions. Are they intentionally being hurtful or being ignorant? It can be very hard to tell in our modern society. Some folks are making very good livings being ignorant and inflammatory and I can't fathom why these people are still allowed in society.

Well actually, I can...

It goes on because people are willing to pull each other down to make themselves look better to others or feel better about themselves. I see it more than I'm comfortable with, especially among people of color. Some of us are willing to be hardcore "Uncle Toms" to get ahead. Many have gone as far as throwing their relatives under the bus. I'm sure you can think of a few examples. Internalized racism is real and dangerous in our communities.

One thing that life has taught me is that the most reliable way to combat negativity is with positivity. It's time to rewrite the long-standing narrative in melaninated communities.

Don't gossip about the single mother down the block. Invite her over and try to connect. That homeless person doesn't need your pity and scorn; they need your support to get back on their feet. Replace those ugly messages with uplifting ones. Building each other up makes us all stronger.

Putting the work off won't change things. Trying to shift the responsibility has gotten us where we are now. As Michael Jackson said; "It's time to make a change."

We are the ones who can make things better. Let's get moving.

The Right Thing

"Why today, Lord? Why now?"

The shouting of protesters could be heard from three blocks away. They had been camped out in front of the county courthouse for several hours now. People were chanting and yelling at passers-by, ruining the peace of an otherwise lovely afternoon in September. I had driven past them several times in hopes that they would leave, but I was usually not that lucky.

I didn't have any business with these people. I simply wanted to pay the fines for my traffic tickets. Unfortunately, I had to cross the picket line to get into the courthouse. It took me around twenty minutes to work up the nerve to proceed with my original plan, instead of just leaving and returning on a more peaceful afternoon. It did me no good to procrastinate about paying my fines out of cowardice. I took a deep breath, lifted my chin, and walked towards the front entrance of the courthouse.

"It's not natural!"

"God doesn't allow it!"

"You are either with us or against us!"

I swallowed hard but kept walking. I didn't want to hear any of this. This wasn't my business, not my fight. I just wanted to pay my debt to society before it got out of hand. Suddenly, just as I approached the bottom of the courthouse stairs, I heard a rather aggressive, male voice call out from the throng surrounding me.

"Hey! You can't just walk past us! We refuse to be ignored!"

I froze on the spot. There was no way that voice wasn't referring to me. If only I was feeling more confident that day. I probably would have just kept walking and ignored him.

Instead, I turned slowly as a heavyset man carrying a "God Hates Fags" sign walked over to me.

"What do you think you're doing?" he roared.

I pointed toward the courthouse above us, so close and yet so far. "Going in there."

"Not today, you aren't," he replied sternly, stepping closer.

My heart dropped. "Why not?" I asked feebly.

The loud man started shaking his finger in the courthouse's direction. "If those bastards think that they can legalize this BLASPHEMY, then NOTHING'S getting done TODAY!!" His skin was beginning to turn a shade of bright red while he yelled.

"Oh." I nodded feebly. There wasn't anything else I could say. My brain was too busy thinking of escape strategies.

"OH! Is that all you have to say? Aren't you pissed off about it? The Government trying to push the gay agenda down our throats." The irate man leaned down towards me, closer to my eye level.

"Umm...well..." was all I could manage. I wasn't pissed off about it at all. In fact, I was glad the government was making this particular decision. It upheld one of the founding principles of this country. People can do whatever they please in the pursuit of happiness, within the confines of the law. The state shouldn't dictate who people could talk to, what they should believe in, or who they could love.

To be honest, I was tired of the entire argument. It didn't make any sense for people to be fighting the way they were. However, I was cornered and pretty sure that the large gentlemen in front of me did not think the same way I did.

"Well, what?" His breath was on my face now. A couple of other protesters had gathered around.

I had to say something. With a sigh, I lifted my chin.

"I don't think there is much of a gay agenda to be worried about. Not unless you have a severe problem with your socks matching your shirts."

Obviously taken aback, the man's eyes widened. "What did you just say?" He looked as if he was going to have a heart attack at any second. There was an audible gasp among the crowd. I took the opportunity to shift my weight to the foot closest to the courthouse doors.

I must have felt the momentum shift because I kept talking. "I could have sworn this was America, land of the free, home of the brave. You have just as much right to stand here and threaten me with your morals as I do to kiss another lady if I please. It's not really hurting anybody so have at it, right?"

My opponent's skin was now approaching a shade of purple as his ire rose. He was obviously not used to anyone standing up for themselves. Especially not people that looked like me. It took him a moment to compose a counterattack.

"Are you saying you're one of them God-damned FAGGOTS?!"

I sighed heavily. "No, sir, but I am saying that you are an idiot." I no longer had the time or the patience to stand around and be yelled at for no reason. Gripping my purse strap for emphasis, I stepped around the now violet gentleman and continued up the stairs. The astonished crowd parted and allowed me to pass freely.

My heart was hammering in my chest so hard; other people could probably hear it. I climbed the stairs quickly, fearing some kind of physical retaliation. Thankfully, it never came. The man only yelled obscenities behind my back, fueled by his supporters.

Once I entered the building, I ducked into the nearest doorway to compose myself. Deep breathing was the only thing I could do to keep from fear crying. I wasn't sure where this new-found boldness had come from or where it had suddenly disappeared to. Hopefully, confrontations like that won't become a habit. I don't think my heart could take it.

Cool It

Heatwave day 3: People have started to lose it. Nobody is in a pleasant mood. At least another four days of 100+ degree temps are expected. Stay hydrated.

Speaking of losing it, don't be that guy.

You know the one.

The guy who always has to offer their opinion when nobody asked for it. The guy who dismisses other people's feelings. The guy who thinks poor people deserve to be poor. The guy who turns up their nose at the gay couple across the room. The guy who believes that their life's success is totally merit-based. The guy who avoids homeless people in the street as if they are contagious. The guy who thinks racism is over and Black people need to stop talking about it.

Stop it. Think about it.

To be like this in the year of Our Lord, 2021…ugh.

It's not a good look.

Disparity

When I was a child, my mother never refused to help anyone that expressed a need. There was always an aunt or cousin staying in our extra room. We fed anyone that came to our door. Family members as well as other people in our neighborhood knew for certain that they could come to our house for a hot meal at least once a week.

I didn't understand why at the time. It wasn't as if we had a whole lot to share. My family was just as poor as every other around us. The thing that made us stand out was our willingness to pool resources. People brought vegetables from their own gardens and various meats and fish that folks came across. That was probably why I didn't realize how deprived I was until I reached adulthood. We poor folks had to stick together to survive. I was brought up to believe that standing alone was no way to live. There could be no happiness if one of us was suffering.

It bothers me that I can do so little to help my fellow man. Every day, I come across another Kickstarter campaign or a GoFundMe page. "One in three campaigns through GoFundMe are for medical costs and the GoFundMe site states they are the leader in online medical fundraising". People have all manner of stories of misfortune and are asking for help. I want to help them all except that I barely have enough to keep my own family from suffering. It's selfish but it is also an act of self-preservation. If I had more to give, I would give it freely. However, I seem to be in the minority in these cases.

I'm sure all of us can name at least one other person that, at one time or another, has fallen into financial despair. Whether the circumstance is one of their own making or the result of the unforeseen, many Americans are only one step away from economic ruin. There is no reason for anyone in the country to be homeless. To be hungry. To be unable to afford healthcare. The United States is one of the wealthiest nations in the world, but these are realities that we face every day. All the wealth in this country is being hoarded by a very small percentage of the population. A percentage that is doing very little to ease the suffering of their fellow Americans.

Corporations have made their way into the government sphere and can influence our lives any way they please. As long as they are seeing a rise in profits, corporations are content to act in their own self-interests. Causing harm to the public or to the plants becomes an afterthought. That isn't to say that some wealthy people are not philanthropic and are willing to do what they can to help people. It just isn't enough to put a dent in the massive financial disparity in our society.

The change we need must begin at the top, so to speak. Those with the power and resources to make lasting changes must be willing to adjust the status quo. People at the bottom can scream, rage, and cry until they can't any longer. Until the wealthy decide that they can no longer sit idly and let people suffer, things will continue along the same path.

As an adult, I try my best to continue with the spirit of giving and community support. I share the tomatoes and peppers from my garden with the neighbors. I keep an eye on the neighborhood kids as they walk past my house towards the corner store. I want more for us, for all of us. If we all tried a little, we could achieve a lot.

"Mama, She Looks Like Me.": The Importance of Black Educators

"When did you first have a Black teacher?"

The question pops up online from time to time and sparks many discussions. The answers tend to vary across socioeconomic lines and regions. Some people encounter Black teachers in elementary school, while others didn't encounter a Black educator until college.

Personally, I didn't run into a Black teacher until high school. Even then, I wasn't enrolled in any of their classes. The Black educators taught in the vocational programs that were still available at the time. In a separate building, as far removed from formal education as physically possible, the Black teachers and their predominately Black students did their thing.

Let's think about this from another perspective. Close your eyes now and imagine a classroom. I bet your description would include desks and bright colors. Maybe even paper, pencils, and crayons. Fresh faced little ones might be sitting on a carpet. Your imagination might even include a teacher in that classroom.

Now that your eyes are open, let me ask a quick question: What does that teacher look like in your imagination? Most folks envision a white woman without thinking. Despite Black women being one of the highly educated groups in America, society still plants education squarely into the hands of white people. Which makes sense seeing as how many of us were subjected to the same treatment as we went through school.

If I've learned one thing over the years, it is that representation matters. Little Black children need older Black

44

people to look up to. They need to see people that look like them achieving in life. These kids need to know that there can be more to life than the circumstances that they were born into. This is part of why so many young Black children want to be ball players, pop stars, or superheroes (Thanks, Chadwick!) when they grow up. Black people are most prominently seen in these areas of mainstream media.

However, there have been some significant strides in representation over the past few years. Barack Obama showed kids that there can be a place for them in politics. Kamala Harris is showing little Black girls that they can have a place in the highest offices in the nation. Amanda Gorman is showcasing the talent and ambition of young Black creatives. Billy Porter is showing queer Black kids that it's okay to be who they are. These are just a few examples of the positive role models that Black children have now.

Having that positive role model does not have to be on a grand scale. The rising number of Black educators lends kids a more accessible goal. You don't have to be rich and to make a difference. Black educators have the added responsibility of caring and supporting children in what can be the most troubling situations of their young lives.

Black teachers serve as a model for Black students in many positive ways. Students can learn how to persevere in the face of adversity, the importance of education, and various other skills from Black teachers. The teachers in question would not have to create any lessons to get their point across either. By showing up for and supporting Black learners, the teachers are modeling positive behaviors that some students do not see anywhere else in their lives.

I'm always amused to see the look of surprise and eventually relief on Black parents' faces when the find out I'll be working with their students. It's almost like, "Okay, it's safe here." Classrooms are not always the safest places for little black kids. It is almost daily that we hear about another egregious tale of indignities forced upon Black students. Just being a presence in the classroom can be a great source of peace for parents and students alike.

The kids appreciate it too. They are quicker to build that relationship with someone who slips out of that teacher voice and into that "mama ain't playing voice" with ease. They can have conversations about cultural happenings easier with someone that looks like them. I can help a little Black girl with her English essay and her Double Dutch game. Little things like that make a world of difference.

It is easier for Black students to relate to a Black teacher. Any good educator can tell you that the key to creating a positive classroom environment are the relationships between the teacher and their students. It is nearly impossible for a student to learn from someone they believe doesn't care about them or their problems. Black teachers can share some lived experiences with their students such as the racism and inequities that exist and hinder so many Black lives. Someone who hasn't lived through growing up Black in this country cannot possibly relate to the pain and trauma of a child going through it now.

Plus, the familiarity of a shared race can open some relational pathways that would be inaccessible for a white teacher. For example, a Black educator would be more likely to understand the slang and jargon of Black youth. Behavior that could be considered violent or threatening to a white educator could be understood to be common horseplay to a Black educator. Misconceptions like this can often lead to stricter discipline being doled out to Black students instead of their white counterparts. Harsher disciping is just another part of the school to prison pipeline that plagues Black students in America. The cultural understanding of Black educators can erase of a lot of unnecessary problems.

It's time to change our perception of Black people in education. We are here and we are mighty. There is already a shortage of teachers in America and the number of Black educators is even less. Encourage Black kids to have careers in education and make learning a priority in the home. It is time to uplift, celebrate and support Black educators for fulfilling such a vital role in the lives of our Black youth.

Guess What?

You don't have to be "evil" or a "bad" person to be a racist or to have prejudices. There are lots of people who consider themselves "good' folks that support racist ideals in their mind. They go to church. They take good care of their families. They would never even dream of being outwardly racist.

But it's there. Deep Down. Only rearing its ugly head during certain moments. You've heard them before.

"Why don't those Black Lives Matter people just relax. All lives are important."

"I don't see race. People are just people."

"Black people should just work harder. They stay poor because of laziness."

"She looks so mean. I bet she would just start screaming if I went up to her."

"All those thugs make me nervous. I don't want that riff-raff in my neighborhood."

"I wouldn't date a black person but I would love to be with one for one night."

"Why do they get to say the N-word and I can't?"

These are just a few examples. All of these statements and those like them are problematic. They don't just come from white people either. Other people of color have racism so deeply internalized that they don't even realize what they're doing. We all need to realize that white supremacy is the bigger issue and come together to defend against it.

The first step to getting past racism…or sexism…or homophobia…or transphobia…or islamophobia…is admitting there is a problem. Nothing gets better by sweeping it under the rug. Denying its existence makes it easier for the most problematic to operate. By saying there isn't a problem, overt racists and the like can further normalize their actions and nothing gets better.

Check yourselves. If you have a question, ask and absorb. Don't get defensive. All of us have things to work on. Make it a priority to inform yourself about issues before speaking on them. Google is only a phone tap away.

We can fix this if we all work together.

Sun and Stars

I love you more than anything.
Your face matches mine, right down to the lines.
You have a big laugh and a bigger heart.
Tall, poofy hair; my sun and stars.
Goofy, helpful, more insightful than you realize.
Such a sweet child, nearly a man grown now.
I have to let you discover your own path
But...
How?
It's not safe for you out there.
The world is unkind to those like us.
Black and young, male in particular
and different from those
who try to confine you with labels
Heaven forbid you have the guts
To stick up for yourself or others like you
The audacity to live as free as you deserve.
There are those who are ready to take you down a peg;
To hold you down
To extinguish your light
My light, my sun and stars.
I never gave birth to a hashtag.
I didn't teach a martyr to read.
I have never rocked a victim to sleep at night
I didn't raise a rallying cry.
I'm afraid; my sun and stars
You're aching for freedom.
It's time, I know
But I can't.
I want you to wait. I want you to slow down.
Stay with me a little longer.

Where I know you are safe.
But...growth doesn't wait.
Life goes on
Your life must go on.
I can't protect you anymore.
Maybe I never could
But it's been fun to pretend.
It's time to let go...
But...
I'm afraid
I'm scared the world will detonate
My sun and stars.
and leave behind
a black hole
I could never escape.

The Stranger

Have you ever felt lonely while being surrounded by others? Many people have called this a strange otherness that they have difficulty living with or describing. I've fallen victim to such feelings myself, more often than I would like. My therapist would blame this phenomenon on my mild anxiety disorder and usually, I would agree, but I've come across some things in my research that would imply that this is a common feeling in society.

There was a classical era sociologist named Georg Simmel. His work covered a broad range of topics from social hierarchies to fashion trends. His name pops up in a variety of different textbooks occasionally. Tonight, however, I'm reminded of his essay called "The Stranger".

In his essay, Simmel speaks of social groups or rather membership in social groups. One of the roles he describes is that of the stranger. The stranger is a member of a social group but remains on the fringes. A person who is generally accepted, but has very loose ties with the other group members. They can drift in and out of or even between groups without much notice.

Think of the traveling merchant of days of old. They would go between different villages and kingdoms to sell their wares. The merchants managed to keep a good enough relationship with their customers to keep their income afloat, but they weren't really included within other social matters of the land.

I'm playing that role this evening. I'm sitting in a room full of middle-aged to elderly, upper-middle-class, white Christians. I'm a member of this church and have been attending for years, but I still feel like I am very much a stranger. It has become much more evident in the age of Trump and his supporters.

I know that includes many members of this congregation. I've heard their ramblings before the election and even afterward. Some of their opinions are very misguided and I'm forced to keep my own thoughts to myself to remain sane with these folks.

It is admittedly a tough place to be in. As I am trying to become a better Christian, I know the value of having a church home and family. At the same time, I question the Christianity of some of the people I'm surrounded by. How could you align yourself with the rantings of such a hateful person? How can you stand idly by while people in your community are suffering? Wasn't that one of Jesus' core teachings, loving your neighbor as you love yourself?

A smart person would just find another church. They would leave and seek the companionship and support of more like-minded people. I, however, am obviously a glutton for punishment. Even now as I type this, I can't bring myself to leave. My family still attends this church and I don't want to leave them behind. Also, my son is beginning to explore his faith and I don't want my issues to impose on any comfort he may have here.

So, I remain a stranger in a very familiar land. The connections I have are few and that circle is becoming smaller as people stronger than I leave on their own journeys. Perhaps, their departure will make my own that much easier.

Dirt Dreams/Leaves and Branches

I visited a mound today.

A mound of Earth that was built by Native Americans around 1100 A.D.

It was hot and the march to the top was exhausting, but I made it. The view from there is impressive, but imagine how it looked when it was new. Before time and industry wore it down. It had to have been amazing.

I thought about how my life would be if I had been born in that era. Working the fields in the same hot sunlight, preserving crops and fish for the brutal winters, birthing countless children without the aid of modern anesthesia. I'm sure I would have accepted it. How would I know any better? I would play the mother's role as my mother and her mother did.

Standing on that mound made me reflect. I thought about all the people that had come before me. Civilizations that have come and gone before I was ever thought of. I thought about people that just went about their day-to-day lives, thinking about the past and future just like I do. Did those native women want to live free and happy lives just like I do? Did they dream of future generations and see greatness? The ancestors laid so much groundwork for us to build on and many of us ignore our historical connections altogether.

Would they be sad to know that? Would the people that came before us be bothered by the way we live now, locked in our own little bubbles?

I asked myself these questions and teared up. I hope I'm making my ancestors proud. I hope they gain the peace of knowing that their struggles and hardships weren't in vain. I hope they are pleased that the legacy they left hasn't been totally erased; that their lives mattered.

I decided, standing there in the summer sun, that I would live out my days in a way that would make my great grandmothers happy. I hope I'm part of the future they were dreaming of.

Later that week, I visited my old home. The property used to belong to my grandparents and I grew up in the house with them, my mom, and my aunts and uncles.

The old house isn't there anymore. My aunt had a new one built and she lives there now. The construction process meant that lots of our old foliage had to go. I'm talking about trees that my grandfather planted. He planted a tree every time one of us was born until he couldn't physically do it anymore. I think mine was the last one. It was a young spruce in the center of the front yard.

The only tree remaining belonged to my grandmother. The story goes that it was a wedding gift. That small gesture grew into the tree planting tradition every time a baby was born in our family. Today, it stands taller than the new house. The tree I used to climb as a child is still thriving; only a little bark damage from three generations of kids playing there.

Storms have taken a branch or two. Erosion has exposed some roots. Nevertheless, the tree is still standing, still blooming every spring. New leaves and boughs growing every year.

The same point could be made about our family. There have been hardships and turmoil. Things that would tear apart those with less secure roots. Despite all that, our family is still here, still growing, still thriving.

My grandmother's tree outlived her and it will probably outlive me. It's amazing to think about how your legacy can live on and change the perspective of your descendants. We should all be mindful of the seeds we are sowing for the future.

Black Girl Rising

My happiness isn't scary or offensive. I can laugh as long and as loud as I please.
You should find some joy of your own.
My pride in myself and my Blackness has nothing to do with you.
Stay out of my way.
The way I move my body is an expression of myself. Fast or slow, I'm gonna go.
Don't judge my groove.
I don't smile because I don't want to. What does that have to do with you?
You aren't the boss of me.
I'm gonna cry. Don't try to stop me. My tears are probably your fault. I'll sob if I wish.
Deal with it.
Let me be angry. Let me get loud. Let me deal with my rage in a healthy way.
Would you still be mad if my skin was lighter?
You don't own me.
Stop trying to contain my emotions. They aren't going anywhere.
Perhaps, you should.

Flower Power

"Keep your face to the sunshine and you
cannot see the shadow. It's what sunflowers
do." – Helen Keller

A few days ago, there was an unexpected break in the weather. Since it was nice enough for walking, I paid a visit to the local botanical garden. The 79-acre space is covered with beautiful and well-maintained plant life. There are locally grown plants as well as those grown in more tropical climates. It was a lovely reminder that Spring had finally arrived, and Summer is just around the corner. Plus, it always improves my mood. Being in nature, surrounded by living things, always manages to make me feel better about life and whatever situation that has been thrust upon me.

I have a great love for gardening. Getting my hands into some mud and helping things grow is an amazing feeling. There's a sense of pride to be had in watching your seeds grow into beautiful flowers. Although fruits and vegetables have more practical uses, I prefer to grow flowers in my garden. I think of them as little bursts of happiness to improve my days.

All species are great in my book, but I have a special affection for Russian Mammoths. There is just something regal and majestic about a bloomed mammoth sunflower. Head still high, before the seeds are formed. Unbowed; Unbroken.

Eventually, the bees and other pollinators do their job and the weight of the seeds becomes too much. Our majestic flower is forced to lower her crown for her offspring to be great in the future. Each flower makes hundreds of tiny flowers inside. Each little flower can become a seed. Seeds that need to be nurtured, although they can survive and thrive even in the harshest of environments.

Flowers provide a sense of beauty and natural comfort to people. The growth and dormancy of many flowering plants serves as a strong reminder of life's cycle of death and rebirth. Sunflowers perform these actions beautifully for many of us.

Sunflowers are super easy to grow and care for and some species are annuals that return to your garden every year. They belong to a group of plants called heliotropes. This means that the younger flowerheads seek out the sun and follow it across the sky.

Have I mentioned that I love sunflowers? Probably. I'll tell anyone who'll listen. Clearly, I'm not the only one. Lots of other Black girls have identified with sunflowers and I think the connection is obvious.

Speaking of young flowers, have you ever watched a group of little black girls at play? They could be jumping rope, playing with each other's hair, or maybe dancing through the spray of a fire hydrant. Their jubilant laughter bringing back memories of your own childhood. One would be hard-pressed to restrain themselves from joining in with these little blossoms while they are flourishing in their joy, basking in the sunlight.

There are so many examples of beautiful Black women in the world. All of us have to remember to keep our heads held high despite the unfair circumstances that life throws at us. Some situations try to break us down, but we remain resilient. Heads held high with pride.

Does any of this sound relatable? I feel that sunflowers tell the story of black people and our ability to keep making a way out of nothing. Our ability to keep blooming within the toughest living conditions imaginable. I have a habit of relating each flower to a mother bringing up her children. A black mother is my vision. Surrounded by children that she has birthed and those she hasn't, the mother provides guidance and protection to her children. My mother comes to mind. She has acted as a caregiver to nearly every small child in her neighborhood. Even as adults, they make time to check in with her. To see how she's doing and to show off how they've grown.

My mother is getting older. She doesn't move quite as fast as she used to, but she is still highly respected in the community. Her kindness over the years has earned her a place of honor among the younger generations. Nobody messes with her. The seeds she nurtured for so long have bloomed into their own healthy crop. Many of us have children of our own. The cycle begins again.

Black Mothers are so much like my Mammoths than anyone may realize. Remember, when things get stormy, to dig your roots deep, hold your head up high and chase the sun!

Through the Looking Glass

I see you, white lady.
I'm not looking right at you, but I can see you.
Are you amused by my husband and me having dinner?
Is it a problem that our skin tones don't match?
or do you like the way I eat this pasta?
The way I add extra red pepper to the "Cajun" noodles?
It's the way my husband eats his boneless chicken, isn't it?
Something has to be very amusing for you to be so...
Invested.
 In our meal and our conversation.
You were certainly watching our mouths like you didn't have
a plate of your own in front of you.
It's lucky for you that I don't have that particular anxiety.
I could eat on stage if I needed to.
The point is...
I see you, white lady.
I see you.

Mental Break

I want to take a minute here to check in. Are you doing okay? We've covered some heavy topics already and the next section can be heavy as well. I wanted to give you a moment to stop and reflect. Does any part of my story resonate so far? Is there anything you need to get off of your heart right now? Maybe there is something or someone you are grateful for. Take this opportunity to write it out. Words have power!

_____
_____
_____
_____
_____
_____
_____
_____
_____
_____
_____
_____
_____
_____
_____
_____
_____
_____
_____
_____
_____
_____

Part 3

FAT

Affirmation

I am capable.
I am deserving of love and respect.
I am willing to do what is needed to achieve my goals.
I am able to accept the good things that happen to me.
I am able to accept the kindness of others.
I am becoming who I'm meant to be.

Look me in the eye

I don't like mirrors. Especially, full-length mirrors. I have one in my house, but it's covered up in a corner of my bedroom. It might be cracked by now; it's been a while since I looked at it. I don't care to find out.

Call it a side effect of having low self-esteem for most of my life.

One of my goals this year is to get past this. I know it's gonna be hard. I've tried before and couldn't handle it.

I want to like how I look. I want to look at myself in that big mirror and not want to break the thing.

It's quite hard since I don't exercise if I can avoid it and I don't drink enough water. I can try to make myself drink more, but it's much harder during my regular workday.

I hate exercise. It starts okay but then I get sore and I want nothing to do with it again.

This is awful and unacceptable. Time to do better.

What this boils down to is that I must make some positive changes to my lifestyle. The problem is that I'm not sure how.

I know motivation is my issue, but it's nearly impossible to motivate myself for any meaningful amount of time. Depression and all, you know.

I also know that it seems like I'm using my mental illness as an excuse. It's hard to try and be healthier when your brain is telling you that it's a waste of time and everyone dies in the end anyway...

Self-improvement is harder when your brain is set up against you. I can take my meds and talk to my therapist exactly as I should, but I'll still defeat myself.

I'm open to suggestions from other folks here. Whatever is working for you. Exercise challenges. Water drinking challenges. Anything motivational that I can look at whenever I feel like I'm getting nowhere. I've looked up a few and will let you guys know how things are going as I progress.

Alternative Lifestyle

Considering my desire to move ahead with my life, I made a decision that had been looming for quite some time.

I decided to have bariatric surgery.

I didn't have a body image issue. I've been fat most of my life and I've been comfortable with it. The problem came in with age. I was getting older and chronic illnesses were creeping around my back stair. Diabetes and heart disease run in my family. It would only be a matter of time if I didn't do something.

I'd tried dieting and exercise before, but I hadn't been able to make any lasting progress. I fall off the wagon and feel worse for even trying. I knew that the surgery would force me to make life changes that were better for me.

Part of that was very daunting. I was nervous about every step in the process up to and including the surgery itself. Change is scary for almost everyone but it's something that must be done.

One can't do better by doing the same things over and over.

I decided to document my process. Maybe it will help someone facing this same decision down the line.

Changes

I started going to therapy consistently in July. I can say that the healing process is messy. Things can get worse before they get better, but you have to commit to doing the work. It's worth it. You're worth it.

It was a daily struggle to live better. Dealing with my depression head-on was the hardest thing I've ever done. Although there were days when I didn't think I could make it, I managed.

Having said that, I did notice the universe was allowing more positive things to come my way. I was starting to embrace a spirit of gratitude and things were moving in a positive direction. Some things I can't discuss right now, but there is a major thing that I can speak on:

A few months ago, I started the process of preparing for bariatric surgery. I didn't have a huge issue with my weight, but I wanted to be healthier. Physically and mentally, I needed to change. I'd been waiting for my insurance to make a decision all that time and I was formally approved for vertical sleeve gastrectomy (VGS) on December 1st.

My surgery date was December 24th and I started my liquid diet 10 days prior.

The purpose of the 10-day liquid diet is to shrink the liver in preparation for surgery. The liver partially covers the stomach and it would be in the way during the procedure. Since the procedure was being done laparoscopically, it would be harder to get around the liver without shrinking.

I was terrified but hopeful.

I know this process is something many people have questions about and I'm willing to use this platform to share my story. Tackling my mental wellness as well as my physical challenges felt daunting, but I knew this was the right decision to make. Hopefully, as usual, I can be useful to someone in their time of need.

My official pre-op weight was 323.6 pounds. Let's see where this trail leads.

Waterlogged

I was going to write a very deep and insightful post about my 10-day, pre-op liquid diet. However, on the last day, my energy level was shot. My instructions were to skip liquid protein supplements for the last 48 hours and I couldn't think very well. My thoughts were sluggish, but I tried to soldier on.

The past ten days had been interesting. My body prepared for the new adjustment as well as I could have expected. The first few days without solid food were hard. I was cranky, irritated, and really wanted a cheeseburger. I couldn't drive around without lusting after every fast-food place I saw. Going to the grocery store became overwhelming. I almost started sobbing in the middle of Walmart on day 3.

Something I feel like I was unprepared for was the liquid poop. I should have put it together before I crossed that bridge. If only liquids go in, only liquids come out. Sometimes, they have an urgent need to come out. My suggestion is to remain near a comfortable bathroom during your liquid phase. You don't want an embarrassing story to add to your weight loss journey.

My relationship with food was changing. At one point, I dreamt that I was eating an entire pan of macaroni and cheese. When I realized I was sabotaging myself, I was upset. Not only after the dream ended, but for the rest of the morning. I was mad about things that never actually happened. Mostly because I knew how easy it would be to ruin all the good I was doing. Just one weak moment and I would set things back for possibly months. I was going to do better.

The last few days, I'd been a slug. The lack of protein was really setting in. I didn't have the energy to do much more than eat popsicles and sleep. I'm sure the rest was good for me, but it did put a damper on Christmas prep. I didn't do much shopping or wrapping that year. I never even put up a tree.

My surgery was in the morning. I'd lost fifteen pounds that week and an additional ten pounds since my surgery journey started in July. I was hopeful that this surgery would be an extremely useful tool for me to get healthier. To improve my life and attitude.

Week One:

Serious Adjustments

I was told that the first four weeks after surgery would be the toughest. It's the warning that all previous bariatric patients echo in support groups across the board. I tried to listen to the warnings and internalize them, but I had no idea what I was getting myself into.

The surgery itself was uneventful. Everything went as it was supposed to. My incisions were clean and I was left with a small port delivering anti-nausea medication just above my stomach. I was scheduled to spend one night in the hospital, but I was having a hard time with sinus drainage. I wasn't sick, but my typical morning runoff was irritating my new stomach. Sneezing and coughing brought nightmarish pain and vomiting up old blood became a regular occurrence.

The first time it happened, I was terrified. I was coughing and having trouble getting air. The nursing staff was amazing and assured me that the blood was probably from the breathing tube used in surgery irritating my throat. It had to go somewhere and back up my throat seemed to be the answer. Scary, but I made it through.

Another thing people warned me about was the gas pain. The surgeons needed to fill my abdomen with gas to perform the surgery and it didn't just go away. It lingered and made me very uncomfortable. Passing gas was impossible until day six. The experts suggested walking around to alleviate some pressure. It helped some, but my energy level wasn't ready to do laps around the hospital all day.

After two nights, I was released. I went home and went right to bed. Resting was important, especially since my body had been deprived of proteins for almost two weeks. Protein helps the healing process and I had been a few days away from sneaking it back into my diet. I was prescribed pain and nausea medicine and sent on my way.

There wasn't a huge amount of post-operation pain or nausea. Most of my incisions were numb. However, the largest one, the one that my stomach was removed through, hurt pretty regularly. A lot of that had to do with my moving around. My abdominal muscles were cut and getting around was interesting while trying not to use them. Every day was better, but the struggle was still real. There was a special kind of helpless feeling when I had to yell for help because I had to use the restroom and I couldn't get up.

The port in my belly needed to be removed on day four. The nurses told me that I could handle it at home. Looking back, it wasn't a big deal but at the time I thought I was gonna pass out.

I was told to work on it in the shower. The warm water and soap would loosen up the surgical tapes and adhesive so I wouldn't tear my skin. It still took quite a bit of coaxing but it did come loose. Finally, I was faced with pulling two tubes out of my belly. The first came out easily. There was about a foot of tubing underneath my skin. It was a crazy feeling. The second didn't want to leave so easily. My mother suggested holding my breath and pulling the tube nonstop until it was out.

After this ordeal, I went straight to bed for the rest of the evening.

They also told me to drink plenty of fluids to prevent dehydration. I really struggled with this. Sixty-four ounces of fluid don't feel like a lot until you can barely swallow a mouthful. I was sipping constantly and I didn't have the patience. I was working on getting back to food with a little more excitement than drinking water.

Another piece of advice that I ignored was eating alone for the first month. I thought this particular warning was silly at the time. Smelling food and watching other people eat didn't bother me before surgery, but it did after. People had been pretty nice about not wanting to eat in front of me, but turning point was when my husband ate a bacon cheeseburger in front of me and I was furious. I was sipping down chicken broth at the time and I wanted to push him down a flight of stairs. I was okay with taking my nibbles alone as long as I didn't get tempted to hurt people I care about.

Weight loss had taken a back seat to healing this week. I wasn't concerned with the scale. I was thinking about yogurt and fluids. I was officially one-week post-op and had started eating cream soups again. I never want to eat plain chicken broth again and I've never looked forward to grits more in my life. Things were still shaky, but light could be seen at the end of the tunnel.

New year, new me indeed.

Week Two:

Sips and Nibbles

This week wasn't very eventful. I was still working on healing after surgery.

I went to my scheduled doctor's visit and he said that I was doing well. My incisions were still looking good. We looked at my new stomach pouch on an x-ray. It was weird. I drank some chalky, white liquid and we watched it move through me. He said that I must have been doing what I was supposed to be because my staples were still holding. I asked if that was a big problem. According to him, people get too excited about eating again and make all manner of bad choices. Sometimes, he has to go back in to repair strictures (narrowing of the new stomach outlet), ulcers, and hernias. Nasty, painful business.

The pain level was very tolerable and I was totally off of pain meds. If I had to compare it to a previous experience, it was similar to my C-section. I had to take my time moving around and be mindful of my belly. If I moved too quickly I would get this twinge of pain, but I handled it with ease.

I also got a little bit better about getting my liquids in. I had a hard time drinking 64 oz. of water before my surgery. At that point, my need to sip slowly had made it even more difficult. However, I'd managed to figure out a little system that kept me from constantly sipping. I would take a mouthful of water and swallow it a little at a time. Yes, I probably looked silly holding water in my cheeks. No, I didn't care what anyone thought about it. My system worked.

Slowly I started eating solids again. Soft foods like oatmeal, grits, yogurt, and applesauce had become staples. I could also have protein shakes. Consuming 50 grams of protein every day was (and is) nearly impossible without meat and beans. My mother and I started looking for creative ways to get protein powder into foods. She found a brand that was supposed to work well in recipes.

The cravings for unhealthy things got better. Not totally gone, but better. I still wanted pasta and pizzas like everyone else. Chips and queso had been my choice comfort food for years. The difference was that I had to convince myself that I didn't want it anymore. Those things would've seriously injured me and I didn't need or want any more surgeries. It had become a literal matter of life and death.

I wanted to skip ahead in my treatment plan and start testing my pouch with different things. I'd managed to eat some mashed potatoes without pain. Steamed veggies were also okay, provided that I chewed them up properly. Those were both technically week three foods, but I was feeling ambitious.

Daily vitamins became a part of my life. I had to incorporate two multivitamins; vitamin C and B12, biotin, and iron into my daily routine. I was worried about this change, but it wasn't too bad. I could work most of my vitamins into morning and evening mealtimes. Sometimes, I would need to sneak one of my calcium gummies into my break when I was at work.

Speaking of work, two weeks post-op and here I was having to report back in. I knew it would take a lot out of me because work wore me out on a normal day before surgery. I was supposed to take three 10-minute walks every day to build up endurance and get some exercise in. I was doing my walks, but it really wore me out. The first week back was an endeavor.

I knew I wasn't supposed to be watching the scale, but it was hard not to. I was there every morning. I surprised myself on New Year's Day. For the first time in over fourteen years, I was hovering between 299 and 300 pounds. I hadn't been down that far since before my son was born. It also meant that

I had lost thirty pounds since December 1st. Both were huge wins for me.

My goal weight was 200 pounds by December 1st, 2019. I didn't think it was possible before, but I had done that much even before getting the gastric sleeve. It felt like a real possibility. I didn't care if I was exactly on the nose, as long as I got close, to me that was a victory. Of course, it would take a lot more work and dedication, but I had come too far to abandon this now.

Week Three:

Two Steps Back

It was a rough one, friends.

I was right to be concerned about going back to work. I had tried to take it easy. To stay still as much as I could, but I don't have that kind of job. I think my doctor misunderstood that when he cleared me to return to work. If I had a desk job, where I could just hang out in a cubicle and sip water and protein shakes all day, going back to work wouldn't have been a big deal. Sadly, that was not my reality.

I have to give a big shoutout here to my work family. They could tell I was pushing myself. I was constantly reminded to sit down and stop trying to do so much. I'm sure I would have come out worse than I did without them.

At the same time, I did fair badly. My pain level had continued to increase throughout the day. By the time the buses pulled away, I could barely walk. My entire torso hurt and I had zero energy. However, I had lived through it. I knew I could handle another day. Things would get easier as time went on.

Incorrect!

The next morning, my body felt like dead weight. Walking to the shower was a herculean feat. By the time I tried to put my pants on, I was panting. I'm sure there would have been sweat if I wasn't wrapped in shower steam. There was no way I was gonna make it.

I have to pull over here to thank my work fam again. They were so understanding and supportive during that whole ordeal. I paid them back for all the love the best way that I could. I made sure they knew what it meant to me.

I made my calls and emails for work and went back to bed. I spent most of my day there. Tomorrow would be better, right?

No. Wrong again!

I'd like to take a moment here to discuss *dumping syndrome*. It can happen to people that have had most of their stomach removed or some other kind of gastric surgery. Symptoms can include abdominal cramps, nausea, vomiting, diarrhea, and lightheadedness. Dumping syndrome generally can happen when food passes too quickly into the lower intestine, usually because of unprocessed sugars in the stomach.

Try to imagine a cramp, okay. Now this cramp begins in your stomach, wages war there for a while, moves up the esophagus, makes you barf, then moves back down your whole GI tract. Your body is in excruciating pain the whole time while all these other things are happening simultaneously. Now imagine this happening over and over, in waves, for several hours. Couple this with the cold sweats and it feels like you might be dying.

That's how I spent most of my Wednesday morning.

I could barely keep anything down. I tried to take my nausea medicine but it always came back up. My mom made me keep sipping water through the whole ordeal. I needed something in my stomach to throw up. Stomach acid isn't great for the esophagus, long term. I eventually managed to keep some pain medicine in me long enough for the waves of agony to pass and I slept for another few hours.

I'm so grateful that my mom has gone through this kind of thing before. She had the gastric sleeve done about eight years ago. According to her, the entire first month after surgery was full of afternoons like mine. I wouldn't have known how to get past anything happening to me without her guidance.

The experts say that I wasn't truly having dumping. My blood sugar was okay at the time. What happened to me was just an advanced round of nausea. Like super nausea. Like, "Please remove the rest of my organs, I don't need them anymore" nausea. I can honestly say that, short of labor and childbirth, it was the worst pain I had ever experienced.

After that ordeal, I decided to stop trying to push myself. I wasn't going back to work that week. My body was simply not having it. I was still not getting enough protein and liquids and I didn't want to push myself back into a hospital bed. I resigned myself to resting as much as possible.

Until Friday...

My mother does some babysitting from time to time. That particular morning, she was watching a six-month-old when she realized that she urgently needed to go to the store. She asked me to keep an eye on the baby while she was gone. I knew she wouldn't be away for long and I didn't mind.

Not smart.

Six-month-old kids like to play this game. It's called "Throw everything on the floor and whine until someone picks it up". Somehow, I forgot all about this and went along with it for a while. They also like to play the "Pick me up, put me down" game. I went along with this too. Until my side started to hurt.

When you have abdominal surgery, or any surgery really, your doctors give you a limit on how much physical activity you are supposed to be doing. This is to keep your body healing the way it is supposed to. I was not supposed to be lifting anything over twenty pounds until the end of February. That included babies.

My large incision and the surrounding area became sore again. It was more painful than I'd like to admit at times. Everything still looked fine, but moving had become more challenging again. Sitting up, sitting down, anything that involved moving my midsection was in danger of sending shooting pains across my middle. I just had to be very delicate with myself until I could heal completely.

That weekend wasn't shaping up to be restful, either. Between funerals and bible study, I was doing more than I should. I knew I needed to settle down but I didn't want to miss things if I didn't have to. I was spending every spare second in bed, taking my vitamins, and trying to remain positive.

That week wasn't one of my best. I knew I had a bad habit of just pushing through pain, but that just wasn't possible. Taking time to heal was essential to my continued health and future success. That's a thing I knew consciously. If only I could make it work in practice.

Week Four:

Govern Yourself Accordingly

Hello, my name is Tangela and I'm a recovering foodaholic.

In the past, I used food as a coping mechanism. I can remember having a particularly bad day. I had gotten some bad news back about a job I was applying for and my grades were not as good as I had expected that semester. Later that afternoon, I ate an entire pepperoni pizza in my car and cried. I would stuff myself to avoid dealing with problematic feelings. The feelings never disappeared; I just gave myself a distraction. In the same way that people use drugs or alcohol to escape, I used pizza and pasta. I've done the work to decrease my dependence over the years and things were much better before I decided on gastric surgery. However, everyone wants to fall off the wagon from time to time.

It can be much harder to spot a food addict. Everybody has to eat. Unless you are very aware of another person's habits, you would miss someone eating their feelings. Plus, eating is a highly social activity. Getting together with friends for appetizers and drinks was one of my favorite things to do. It is very hard to plan some kind of social outing without including a meal. To many, this might not seem to be an issue but consider this:

When people eat together, bad habits are rampant. Unless you are determined to stay focused on your goals, eating healthy is more difficult. The temptation to order something fried, cheesy, or carb-loaded is in full effect. At the same time, people tend to eat faster while talking. Eating faster makes your stomach full faster. So much faster that your brain doesn't register that you've had enough when it happens.

Most folks keep eating, distracted, until it becomes uncomfortable. That's a bad time for anybody.

There have been times, before my surgery, that my friends and I would go on late night appetizer runs. A bunch of local restaurants and bars have happy hour or late-night food deals. We would hop from place to place and just eat unhealthy amounts of mozzarella sticks and onion rings. The hot wings felt endless. Couple this with alcohol, and the poor decision making wasn't always limited to food. The days following these escapades were usually filled with nausea, stomach pain, and general anger at myself for acting like an idiot. However, I never turned down the opportunity to gorge myself in the name of a good time.

Since I started my wellness journey, I incorporated mindfulness into my eating. This is a technique that can improve your regular eating habits by reducing how much you take in, thus lowering calories. This is a sample of my process:

- Not drinking anything 30 minutes before or after meals.
- Taking smaller bites.
- Putting forks and spoons down while chewing.
- Chewing until the food is the consistency of toothpaste.
- Being aware of the signals that my body is sending to my brain to stop.

I started losing weight even before having the surgery using this model. It took a little time to adjust. Old habits don't go down without a fight. This is part of why dieticians suggest eating alone for the first week or two after surgery. Forgetting this process can lead to serious discomfort and possible injury.

Speaking of discomfort and injury, during this week I had also fully returned back to work.

It wasn't too bad. I had managed to work without too much pain or exhaustion. It's hard to take it easy in my line of work. Lifting and jogging could be part of my day to day without warning. Being able to take a punch without reacting is also a perk of the job. During this return, I tried to not exert much force on my midsection. It did feel much better, but I hadn't been medically cleared to do any lifting or vigorous activity. I guess I'd put myself on light duty. As much as I could, anyway.

Part of my good feeling came from getting control of my vitamin regimen. I have to take supplements every day for the rest of my life. Calcium, B12, multivitamins, and occasional iron had become a part of my daily routine. My doctors told me I would have to take them before surgery, but I didn't understand the serious need.

It took a little time for me to get my act together. I acted like I hadn't just had 80% of my stomach removed. It wasn't until I realized I needed the vitamins to have enough energy to get through normal activities that I understood the gravity of these instructions. I couldn't even walk through a store without needing a two-hour nap afterward. The pain was a constant companion and I didn't think I was healing properly. My stubbornness may have set me back a week or two in my progress. My fault. You live and you learn.

The worst part of this week was the encounter with constipation. No one really wants to think about it, but it happens. Especially after your internal operations have been heavily altered and your body is still trying to make sense of it. I had been on a liquid diet for so long, I kinda forgot that pooping was something I was supposed to be doing.

I didn't notice until the number on the scale stopped moving downwards. Several days went by and I had gained a couple of pounds. I couldn't come up with a reason why until the pain started. A low-grade ache turned into something that required pain medication to tolerate. I tried a laxative, but it didn't have the desired result. Instead, I got a night full of excruciating cramps and no fecal removal.

The following day, I turned to coffee. It had always done the trick in the past and it didn't disappoint me now. It took a bit longer than a few hours, but it got the desired result. I made it a point to drink a cup or two of black coffee every day from that point on.

In other news, my depression had taken a backseat. I had been so focused on my physical health that depression hadn't had a leg to stand on. However, a night or two of anxious insomnia were the only dark spots in those last few weeks.

There was a break in the weather and so I took that as a sign to push myself to be more positive. Positive thinking, speaking, and acting had been my mantra. I gave myself some long-term goals that felt very attainable. At the same time, I gave myself hope. My therapist was always talking about the importance of having some hope in your life. Having something to cling to in times of trouble could act as a floating log in the sea of sadness. It could also keep you focused on finding your way to shore instead of allowing yourself to drown.

Getting compliments had also done wonders for me. I always had a hard time accepting positive comments about myself. Since people had started to noticed my weight loss, everyone had been saying how good I looked. There's a message about the negative connotations of fatness in there, but I chose to put those thoughts aside.

My self-esteem was beginning to change as well. Before surgery, it was a struggle to look at me in the mirror. Afterwards, I always wanted to see how my body was changing. Body positivity is harder as a fat girl. I don't think I'll ever see myself otherwise. In my head, I'm gonna be fat for life. Learning to like my fatness has always been hard, but it got a little easier. I was close to my January weight goal with almost two weeks to go. I needed to get my goals and intentions ready for February. If I prepared them right away, everything would be ready to go when the new month started. I would advise everyone to always plan ahead.

Week Five:

Keep It Moving

I reached one calendar month post-surgery on the 24th of January. It was and was not a major milestone. Keeping myself alive and healthy that far was wonderful, but I didn't realize the date had passed until a couple of days later.

I was busy, okay!

Working took up a lot of my time, as usual. In addition to this, I was trying to incorporate more exercise into my day-to-day life. I walked more during the day and did some arm and chest flexing in the evenings. My son and I enjoyed taking walks when we still had some sunlight left. It was harder when the weather was nasty. I usually didn't have the time to drive to the gym. Exercise fell by the wayside on those evenings.

For the record, I had always loathed exercise for the sake of exercise. I loved playing sports and playing around with kids and friends, but making a whole separate trip to the gym was too much. I was too busy and lazy to make that happen.

Going to the gym wasn't always a positive experience for me either. People tended to give the new fat person in the gym large amounts of side-eye. Given my naturally elevated anxiety levels, I could always feel myself being judged. Every time, I got on a treadmill there would be some physically fit person nearby running their fifteenth mile. I only managed a half hour before I couldn't take anymore. Meanwhile, the nearby fit person just finished mile thirty-two and shows no signs of stopping. This made me feel worthless.

All of these problematic thoughts led me away from the gym. I still paid for the membership every month, harboring delusions that I would return. In reality, I was more likely to spend my free time taking cat naps.

I had to find a way to get past these feelings. Exercise isn't the enemy I thought it was. Yes, it still hurts at times. Yes, I get sore and stiff for days afterward. Yes, people still give me unpleasant looks at the gym. At the same time, I promised myself I was going to work on improving. I can't get better by doing the same things I've always done.

Therapy has helped me in so many ways. I've learned the type of messages I should be telling myself to get ahead, to move forward instead of wallowing in my sadness. There were a variety of coping mechanisms that were centered on positive self-talk at the time. I deserved to love myself. I had the right to do what was right for me without judgement. I valued myself enough to be healthy. It was extremely difficult for me to shift my mindset. To this day, positive self-talk is my primary goal.

Talking about my various insecurities also helped to weed out my irrational thoughts. I used to say and think terrible things about myself. Things I would never say about another person. However, my therapist taught me about my inner child. The idea is to imagine my inner self as the person I was when I was six. My job as adult self's task is to take care of her and to treat her kindly. "Would I say those terrible things to a six-year-old? No? Then, stop." Simple as that. Things began to turn around, but progress was slow.

Gym time became a necessary evil. I had to burn off a lot of fat to reach my goal. Sitting around and crying all the time was not the way to get it done. I increased my treadmill time and I wanted to get back to weightlifting. There was some toning and sculpting I wanted to do as well. I lifted for a little while in high school, but it fell by the wayside, as things do when you get older.

I'd also started to eat less than a 1000 calories per day. That didn't seem like much but it could be a struggle to get that far at times. My breakfast included coffee and Chobani blended yogurt cups. Lunch was chicken breast or refried beans and crackers. If I got to dinner, I had some type of steamed veggie and a slice of lean meat. Chicken or fish, most of the time.

The scale wasn't moving much then. I was stuck for a little while. I know that stalls in weight loss are normal, but it is still be very frustrating when you have been doing everything right. However, you shouldn't get inside your head about it.

At that point, I was doing well. Losing 40 pounds in fifty days was amazing. I was focused on my long-term success for the first time in years. I had moments when I got really down on myself because I felt like I could have been doing more. However, I had people to remind me that everything was fine and I was fine. A good support system is invaluable during this process.

Love of Self/Drop it Low

We are told that we shouldn't allow our happiness to be dependent on someone else. That we must be content within ourselves before we can accept love from another. This sounds well and good. Self-love is important and a valid goal to have. However, if you are fortunate enough to find someone who truly cares about you, they will help you to see yourself the way they see you. Flaws and all.

- Despite your bad self-esteem.
- Despite your weird laugh.
- Despite your terrible skin problems.
- Despite your inability to manage time properly.

The right person will love every hair on your wretched little body.

And you won't be able to understand why. It may even make you angry at times. You'll become desperately frustrated that they don't know why you are so awful.

At the same time, you don't want them to. A rational person would leave, for sure. They would use their energy on someone as wonderful as they are.

However, loving eyes can rarely see. Rose-colored glasses and all that.

Having someone who wholly loves you is a life-changing experience. I would hope that everyone could feel this way at some point in their lives, the longer the better. And while I'm on the subject of love. I recently discovered that I like to dance. Like, a lot.

I've been dancing on my own forever. Whenever I hear the right song or a good beat, I can't help myself. However, I don't go out and dance very often. I've been afraid of being laughed at and judged. You may not have noticed, but I'm a fat girl. Have been for years.

I've got quite a bit of extra jiggle when I move my body. Most people can't handle seeing it. It's taken years for me to handle feeling it. People can be quite rude to fat girls. We can't do anything without ridicule. Want to be a fashionista? Not without a healthy budget and very hard to find fashionable options.

Okay then. I'll try to work out? Nope. You'll get made the butt of jokes around the gym. You won't want to step foot in the place again.

I want a fun and varied choice of sexual partners. Sorry. Sexism, slut-shaming, and fatphobia are all working against you here. It's ridiculous!

Heaven forbid you have the audacity to laugh in the face of the haters and do you regardless. It makes people so mad to see a big girl loving herself. People can only direct their attention to Lizzo to see that.

Lizzo is a fat girl who is over your negative opinion about her body and her lifestyle. She is extremely vocal about self-love and self-acceptance in her music and on her social media platforms. Lizzo regularly speaks about how important it is to love your body, no matter what image it is serving at the time. She lives her life as an example to young fat girls that they don't have to be built like fenceposts to feel valuable and desirable. And it drives people nuts!

She has shut down her Instagram comments on numerous occasions when the vitriol became too thick to navigate. People have complained to the FCC about her live performances and the clothes she wears to award shows. That her lyrics and her dancing aren't acceptable. Ask yourself why that is?

Why are people so uncomfortable with seeing fat girls having a good time and encouraging others to do the same. Fatphobia and a certain degree of shame definitely come into play.

When I say shame, I mean that they want us to be ashamed. We should not be proud of the bodies that are obviously out of control. This is when most of them bring up our unhealthy eating or lifestyle habits. We should be ashamed to let the fupa hang out or to let our arm wings see the sunlight. We should be mortified if anyone catches a glimpse of a fat roll. To that Lizzo and I say, "Not my problem."

The good sis continues to put out bops and preaching the good word of self-acceptance. And I will continue to dance. If she can twerk in public, then so can I. But can a big girl just grind on some folks in the club without getting nasty side-eye from literally everyone?

Damn. Can I live?

Conclusion:

Storm Chasing

There are few things I enjoy more than a thunderstorm.

I know a loud storm is unnerving for lots of people. It can be quite scary. My husband and I aren't those types of people. One of our life goals is to become storm chasers when we retire. If we're going out anyway, it may as well be while doing what we love.

Thunderstorms are energizing for us. Watching the clouds mirror the water as they roll across the sky is just thrilling. When most people are heeding the forecasters' warnings to seek shelter, we can usually be found watching the sky in our front yard or enjoying the rain from our porch.

It was a stormy weekend in late June. What people like to call "Tornado Season" in the Midwest. We didn't have any real plans so I was genuinely surprised when my husband suggested a quick road trip to celebrate our wedding anniversary. Our budget gets very tight during the summer and I hadn't made any real plans to celebrate. He wanted to visit his family and get us away from home for at least one night.

I was skeptical at first. Visiting his parents usually involved us sitting around their home for hours while I felt more and more out of place by the minute. He promised that this time would be different, we wouldn't take our son, and we would take a little time for ourselves. The fact that he'd thought that far ahead impressed me. I agreed, and we were on our way.

Our little excursion started very normally. Traffic didn't become an issue until we approached our destination. The weather was hot, but not unbearable. His family was glad to see us, and we did manage to have a private evening to ourselves. All in all, a good anniversary. Things didn't get exciting until we were driving home.

My mother sent a text saying that she was stuck at the church. The sirens were going off and they were all taking cover in the basement. I replied that I wasn't home yet and that there wasn't much I could do about it. I told my husband about the storm and checked the radar on my phone. There was a massive thunderstorm rolling across the state. It covered several counties at a time and we were driving straight into it.

I wasn't worried. We both love a good storm and the energy of a storm can be exhilarating. Most folks say we are crazy, but we don't mind. There is nothing like the feeling of being engulfed in nature's fury.

We had at least an hour before we hit the storm. I suggested taking an alternate route, but he talked me out of it. This storm was standing between us and home. There was no avoiding it.

The drive was uneventful until we reached it. We could see a clear line in the sky between good weather and bad weather. Puffy cumulonimbus clouds became daunting altostratus as we drove. The storm front was dark and tall. The sky behind was dark and unreadable. The winds picked up sharply just before the rain happened. It seemed as if the sky opened and threw buckets of water at us.

Many other drivers had taken refuge beneath overpasses, hoping to wait out the storm. I asked my husband if he wanted to stop driving. He asked me if I wanted him to stop at the same time. Our simultaneous "no" caused both of us to laugh as we pressed on.

The sky continued to put on a show. Lightning was illuminating the otherwise blackened highway. It split apart the clouds and the wind and rain were unrelenting. The sky itself was displaying colors that I'd never seen. Neon greens and intimidating magentas were dancing like fireworks overhead. It was terrifyingly exhilarating.

The rain and wind died down after about twenty minutes. The clouds and lightning were still giving people a good show and we continued driving. I didn't hear any sirens or see any reports, but I feel like we were very near a tornado. You can't convince me otherwise.

As we pressed on, the sun was sinking below the cloud line. Blazing reds and golds joined the majestic greens and blues in the sky. Everything above us was a beautiful, natural gradient. Pictures could never do it justice. As the sun was finally setting, its light turned everything around us into shadows. Imagine the opening scene of The Lion King but in reverse. It was miraculous and glorious. I remember tearing up a little at the sight. My husband grinned as if he'd won the lottery and rubbed my thigh as he drove.

The damage we rode past was just as intimidating as the storm itself. The highway was closed as we neared home and we were forced to take a backroad detour. The destruction was easier to see, despite night having fallen. The road was totally dark except for a few farms with their own generators. My husband had to be more careful with his driving because of fallen branches in the streets. The detour added nearly an hour to our drive and we were exhausted when we got home.

Despite all the chaos surrounding us, it was the most fun experience that we've had as a couple in years. We were both in awe of the raw power that surrounded us, and we laughed like grade-schoolers when the danger had passed. We'd lived to see another sunset. It was freeing; exhilarating. Riding with the storm as it tore across the state was an amazing experience. It was the way I wanted to spend my golden years. Riding through thunderstorms with my husband behind the wheel, watching the sky and the radar by his side.

Ending Thoughts

I've collected these poems and essays as a testament to my resilience. I was really going through some troubling times. I don't point them out just to say that my life is trash. I'm celebrating the fact that I'm still here. I'm still pushing forward despite what was trying to hold me back. I've come a long way since many of these entries were written. I've been doing the work of self-healing and introspection and reaping the benefits of this practice. Revisiting them is a reminder to myself to keep showing up for the girl in this book. To keep standing up and looking out for her happiness and wellbeing. No one else is going to, after all.

I said in the beginning that I want this book to be a help to others. I've laid my struggles out for the world to see and it is okay. I'm still okay. People are allowed to be vulnerable. It doesn't make you less of a person to admit you need help or that you were wrong. There's a type of strength in vulnerability that is admirable. There is a freedom in being who you truly are, unapologetically. I want to be an example of that strength. I want to show the world that we all have battles to fight and they can be conquered with the right mindset and behaviors. The growth you seek is available if you are willing to do the work.

Finally, I want to say a huge thank you to the people in my life that have been pushing me to keep writing. My family members and friends that were irritating to no end about getting my words to the public. I took the leap and finally did it.

Y'all have to find something else to talk about now.

Bibliography

[1] McClanahan, Carolyn. "People Are Raising $650 Million on GoFundMe Each Year To Attack Rising Healthcare Costs." 18 August 2018. Forbes Magazine. 22 May 2021.

60516856R10069